LIQUID

Crafting Excellence: A Complete Handbook for Liquid Soap Making - Master Techniques, Troubleshooting Tips, Business Insights, and More

NATALIE J. FITZPATRICK

TABLE OF CONTENT

CHAPTER ONE
INTRODUCTION TO LIQUID SOAP
MAKING

1.1 Overview of Liquid Soap

Liquid soap is a versatile cleansing product that has gained popularity for its convenience and effectiveness. Unlike traditional bar soap, liquid soap is in a liquid form, making it easy to dispense and use for various purposes. It is made through a process called saponification, where oils or fats react with an alkali substance, such as sodium hydroxide (lye), to form soap molecules.

One of the key advantages of liquid soap is its ability to be customized to meet specific needs and preferences. Manufacturers can adjust the ingredients, fragrances, and additives to create a wide range of formulations tailored to different skin types and preferences. This versatility has contributed to the widespread popularity of liquid soap in both household and commercial settings.

Liquid soap is commonly used for handwashing, body washing, and even as a shampoo or household cleaner. Its liquid form allows for easy application and distribution, making it suitable for use in various contexts, including homes, workplaces, schools, and healthcare facilities.

In addition to its cleansing properties, liquid soap often contains moisturizing ingredients to help prevent dryness and irritation. Many formulations also include antibacterial agents to effectively kill germs and bacteria, promoting better hygiene and reducing the risk of illness.

Overall, liquid soap offers a convenient and effective solution for personal hygiene and cleanliness. Its versatility, ease of use, and ability to be customized make it a popular choice for consumers and manufacturers alike.

1.2 Benefits of Making Your Own

Making your own liquid soap offers a range of benefits, both practical and personal. Here are some key advantages:

1. Control over Ingredients: When you make your own liquid soap, you have full control over the ingredients used in the formulation. This allows you to avoid harsh chemicals, artificial fragrances, and other potentially harmful additives commonly found in commercial products.

2. Customization: Homemade liquid soap can be customized to suit your specific preferences and needs. You can choose the types of oils, fragrances, and additives to create a product that meets your individual requirements, such as sensitive skin or particular scent preferences.

3. Cost-Effectiveness: In many cases, making your own liquid soap can be more cost-effective than purchasing commercial products, especially if you buy ingredients in bulk or grow your own herbs and botanicals for use in formulations.

4. Environmental Sustainability: By making your own liquid soap, you can reduce your environmental impact by using natural, biodegradable ingredients and minimizing packaging waste. Additionally, homemade products often require less energy and resources to produce compared to mass-produced alternatives.

5. Creative Expression: Liquid soap making can be a creative and enjoyable hobby that allows you to express your creativity through experimenting with different ingredients, colors, and scents. It can also be a fun activity to share with friends and family.

6. Personal Satisfaction: There is a sense of satisfaction that comes from creating something with your own hands. Making your own liquid soap allows you to take pride in your craftsmanship and enjoy the satisfaction of using a product that you made yourself.

Overall, making your own liquid soap offers a range of benefits, from control over ingredients to cost-effectiveness and personal satisfaction. It's a rewarding and environmentally-friendly alternative to store-bought products.

1.3 Getting Started

Getting started with liquid soap making requires some basic equipment, ingredients, and knowledge of the saponification process. Here's what you need to begin:

Necessary Equipment

1. Stainless Steel or Heat-Resistant Plastic Containers: For mixing and heating ingredients.

2. Thermometer: To monitor the temperature of the ingredients during the saponification process.

3. Stick Blender: For emulsifying the oils and lye mixture.

4. Protective Gear: Including gloves, goggles, and a long-sleeved shirt to protect against contact with lye.

5. Molds: To shape and form the liquid soap as it solidifies.

6. Measuring Tools: Such as a scale and measuring cups/spoons for accurate measurement of ingredients.

7. Stirring Utensils: To mix the ingredients thoroughly.

Basic Ingredients:

1. Oils and Fats: Such as olive oil, coconut oil, or palm oil, which are the primary components of the soap.

2. Lye (Sodium Hydroxide): An essential ingredient that reacts with the oils to form soap through the saponification process.

3. Water: Used to dissolve the lye and create the lye solution.

4. Fragrances and Additives: Optional ingredients such as essential oils, herbs, or colorants to enhance the scent and appearance of the soap.

Safety Precautions:

1. Work in a Well-Ventilated Area: Ensure good airflow to prevent inhalation of fumes produced during the saponification process.

2. Wear Protective Gear: Gloves, goggles, and a long-sleeved shirt to protect against accidental splashes of lye.

3. Handle Lye with Caution: Lye is a highly caustic substance and can cause burns if it comes into contact with skin or eyes. Always add lye to water (not the other way around) and handle it with care.

4. Follow Recipes Carefully: Accurate measurement and adherence to recipes are crucial for successful soap making.

Once you have gathered your equipment and ingredients and familiarized yourself with the safety precautions, you're ready to begin making your own liquid soap. Start with a simple recipe and gradually experiment with different oils, fragrances, and additives to create your own unique formulations.

CHAPTER TWO
UNDERSTANDING INGREDIENTS

2.1 Essential Components

In liquid soap making, several key components play vital roles in the formulation and effectiveness of the final product. Understanding these essential components is crucial for creating high-quality liquid soap. Here are the primary components:

1. Oils and Fats: Oils are the foundational ingredient in liquid soap making, serving as the base for the soap formulation. Common oils used include olive oil, coconut oil, palm oil, castor oil, and sweet almond oil. Each type of oil contributes different properties to the soap, such as cleansing, lathering, moisturizing, and hardness. Balancing the types and proportions of oils is essential for achieving the desired characteristics in the finished soap.

2. Lye (Sodium Hydroxide): Lye is a strong alkali that reacts with the oils in a process called saponification to form soap molecules. It is a crucial component in soap making, as it is responsible for transforming the oils into soap. However, lye is highly caustic and must be handled with extreme care. Proper safety precautions, such as wearing protective gear and working in a well-ventilated area, are essential when handling lye.

3. Water: Water is used to dissolve the lye and create the lye solution, which is then mixed with the oils to initiate the saponification process. The amount of water used in the formulation can affect the texture, hardness, and curing time of the soap. It's essential to use distilled or filtered water to avoid impurities that can affect the quality of the soap.

4. Additives: Additives are optional ingredients that can be incorporated into the soap formulation to enhance its properties, scent, color, or visual appeal. Common additives include essential oils, fragrance oils, herbs, botanicals, clays, exfoliants (such as oatmeal or ground coffee), and colorants. Additives allow soap makers to customize their formulations to meet specific preferences and needs.

5. Fragrances: Fragrances are often added to liquid soap to impart pleasant scents and enhance the overall sensory experience. Essential oils, which are derived from natural plant sources, are a popular choice for adding fragrance to liquid soap due to their natural aromas and therapeutic properties. However, fragrance oils, which are synthetic fragrances specifically formulated for use in soap making, are also commonly used.

Understanding and carefully selecting these essential components is key to creating high-quality liquid soap that meets your desired specifications and preferences.

2.2 Types of Oils and Additives

In liquid soap making, the choice of oils and additives plays a significant role in determining the properties and characteristics of the final product. Here are some common types of oils and additives used in liquid soap making:

Types of Oils:

1. Olive Oil: Olive oil is a popular choice for liquid soap making due to its moisturizing properties and mildness. It produces a gentle and creamy lather, making it suitable for sensitive skin.

2. Coconut Oil: Coconut oil is valued for its cleansing and lathering properties, producing a rich and bubbly lather in liquid soap. However, it can be drying if used in high concentrations, so it is often blended with other oils.

3. Palm Oil: Palm oil contributes to the hardness and stability of liquid soap, resulting in a longer-lasting bar. It also produces a creamy lather and adds moisturizing properties to the soap.

4. Castor Oil: Castor oil is known for its humectant properties, attracting moisture to the skin and helping to maintain hydration. It also contributes to the lather and stability of liquid soap.

5. Sweet Almond Oil: Sweet almond oil is lightweight and easily absorbed by the skin, making it suitable for moisturizing liquid soap formulations. It helps to soften and condition the skin, leaving it feeling smooth and hydrated.

Types of Additives:

1. Essential Oils: Essential oils are natural plant extracts that are used to add fragrance and therapeutic properties to liquid soap. They come in a wide range of scents, each with its own unique aroma and potential benefits for the skin and senses.

2. Fragrance Oils: Fragrance oils are synthetic fragrances specifically formulated for use in soap making. They offer a wide variety of scents that may not be available in essential oils and are often more affordable.

3. Herbs and Botanicals: Herbs and botanicals can be added to liquid soap for their aesthetic appeal as well as their potential skin benefits. Popular choices include lavender buds, calendula petals, chamomile flowers, and rosemary leaves.

4. Clays: Clays, such as kaolin clay or bentonite clay, can be added to liquid soap for their absorbent and detoxifying properties. They can help to cleanse and clarify the skin by removing impurities and excess oil.

5. Colorants: Colorants, such as natural micas, pigments, or oxides, can be used to add color to liquid soap. They allow soap makers to create visually appealing products in a wide range of hues.

When selecting oils and additives for liquid soap making, it's essential to consider their properties, benefits, and compatibility with your desired formulation. Experimenting with different combinations and ratios can help you create unique and effective liquid soap formulations.

2.3 Quality Considerations

Creating high-quality liquid soap requires attention to detail and careful selection of ingredients and processes. Here are some key quality considerations to keep in mind:

1. Ingredient Quality: Start with high-quality ingredients, such as pure oils, lye, and additives. Choose organic, unrefined, and cold-pressed oils whenever possible to ensure maximum freshness and potency.

2. Proper Formulation: Use accurate measurements and follow recipes carefully to achieve the desired balance of oils, lye, and water in your liquid soap formulation. Proper formulation is essential for creating soap with the right cleansing, lathering, and moisturizing properties.

3. Saponification Process: Monitor the saponification process closely to ensure that the oils and lye are fully reacted and incorporated into the soap mixture. Use a thermometer to track the temperature and observe the stages of saponification, including trace and gel phase.

4. Curing Time: Allow your liquid soap to cure properly before use to ensure that it has fully solidified and stabilized. Curing time can vary depending on the formulation and environmental conditions but typically ranges from several weeks to a few months.

5. pH Balance: Test the pH of your liquid soap to ensure that it falls within the appropriate range for skin-friendly products (typically between 8 and 10). Adjustments may be necessary to achieve the desired pH balance using citric acid or borax solution.

6. Sensory Appeal: Pay attention to the scent, texture, and appearance of your liquid soap to ensure that it meets your sensory preferences and expectations. Experiment with different fragrances, colors, and additives to create unique and appealing products.

7. Packaging and Storage: Store your liquid soap in suitable containers, such as opaque or tinted bottles, to protect it from light and air exposure, which can degrade the quality of the product over time. Proper packaging and storage help to preserve the freshness and effectiveness of your liquid soap.

By adhering to these quality considerations and maintaining high standards throughout the soap making process, you can create liquid soap that is safe, effective, and enjoyable to use.

CHAPTER THREE
EQUIPMENT AND SAFETY PRECAUTIONS

3.1 Necessary Tools

To embark on your liquid soap making journey, having the right tools is paramount. These tools facilitate the soap-making process and contribute to the overall efficiency and safety of your endeavor. Here's a breakdown of the essential tools:

1. Stainless Steel or Heat-Resistant Plastic Containers: These are used for measuring, mixing, and heating ingredients. Stainless steel is preferred for durability and ease of cleaning.

2. Thermometer: Essential for monitoring the temperature of your ingredients during the saponification process. Accurate temperature control is crucial for successful soap making.

3. Stick Blender: A versatile tool for emulsifying the oils and lye mixture. It accelerates the saponification process and ensures a smooth consistency.

4. Protective Gear: Including gloves, goggles, and a long-sleeved shirt. These protect against accidental splashes of lye, ensuring the safety of the soap maker.

5. Molds: Used for shaping and forming the liquid soap as it solidifies. Silicone molds are popular for easy removal and flexibility.

6. Measuring Tools: A scale and measuring cups or spoons for precise measurement of ingredients. Accurate measurements are essential for successful soap making.

7. Stirring Utensils: Utensils like spatulas or spoons for mixing ingredients thoroughly. Choose non-reactive materials to avoid unwanted chemical reactions.

Having these tools on hand sets you up for a smooth and efficient soap-making process, allowing you to focus on crafting the perfect liquid soap.

3.2 Safety Measures

Safety is paramount in the soap-making process, especially when dealing with caustic substances like lye. Implementing proper safety measures ensures a secure environment for soap makers. Here's a comprehensive guide:

1. Work in a Well-Ventilated Area: Adequate ventilation is crucial to dissipate fumes produced during the saponification process. This helps prevent inhalation of potentially harmful substances.

2. Wear Protective Gear: Use gloves, goggles, and a long-sleeved shirt to shield against accidental splashes of lye. This protective gear is non-negotiable for the safety of the soap maker.

3. Handle Lye with Caution: Lye is highly caustic and can cause burns. Always add lye to water (not the other way around) to minimize the risk of splashing. Handle lye with care, and in case of contact, rinse immediately with plenty of water.

4. Follow Recipes Carefully: Accurate measurement and adherence to recipes are critical. Deviating from recommended quantities can affect the outcome and safety of the soap.

5. Work Methodically: Plan your steps and follow a systematic approach. This minimizes the risk of errors and ensures a controlled soap-making process.

By prioritizing safety measures and being vigilant throughout the soap-making process, you create a secure environment for crafting liquid soap while minimizing potential risks.

This detailed exploration provides an in-depth understanding of essential components, types of oils and additives, quality considerations, necessary tools, and safety measures for successful liquid soap making.

CHAPTER FOUR
BASIC LIQUID SOAP MAKING PROCESS

4.1 Step-by-Step Instructions

Making liquid soap involves a series of steps that need to be followed carefully to ensure a successful outcome. Here's a detailed guide on how to make liquid soap:

Step 1: Prepare Your Workspace

- Choose a well-ventilated area with a flat surface to work on.

- Gather all necessary equipment and ingredients.

- Put on your protective gear, including gloves, goggles, and a long-sleeved shirt.

Step 2: Measure Ingredients

- Weigh out the oils and fats according to your recipe using a scale.

- Measure out the correct amount of water needed for the recipe.

- Carefully measure the lye using a scale and handle it with caution, following safety guidelines.

Step 3: Mix the Lye Solution

- In a heat-resistant container, carefully add the lye to the water while stirring gently.

- Stir until the lye is completely dissolved, and the solution is clear.

- Allow the lye solution to cool to around 100-110°F (38-43°C) while stirring occasionally.

Step 4: Prepare the Oils

- Heat the oils and fats in a separate container until they are melted and reach a temperature of around 100-110°F (38-43°C).

- Stir the oils occasionally to ensure they are evenly heated.

Step 5: Combine the Lye Solution and Oils

- Slowly pour the lye solution into the melted oils while stirring continuously.

- Use a stick blender to mix the ingredients thoroughly until they reach trace, a stage where the mixture thickens and leaves a trail or "trace" when the blender is lifted.

Step 6: Add Fragrances and Additives (Optional)

- Once the soap reaches trace, you can add any fragrances, essential oils, colorants, or other additives according to your recipe.

- Stir the additives into the soap mixture until they are evenly distributed.

Step 7: Pour into Molds

- Pour the soap mixture into molds of your choice.

- Tap the molds gently on the countertop to remove any air bubbles and ensure the soap fills the molds evenly.

Step 8: Cure the Soap

- Allow the soap to cool and harden in the molds for 24-48 hours.

- After this initial cooling period, unmold the soap and cut it into bars or transfer it into dispensers for liquid soap.

- Place the soap bars or liquid soap containers in a cool, dry area to cure for 4-6 weeks, allowing excess moisture to evaporate and the soap to harden fully.

Step 9: Test and Use

- Once cured, test the pH of the soap to ensure it falls within the desired range (typically between 8-10 for liquid soap).

- Your homemade liquid soap is now ready to use! Enjoy the satisfaction of using a product that you made yourself.

4.2 Troubleshooting Tips

Even with careful preparation, issues may arise during the liquid soap making process. Here are some common problems and troubleshooting tips:

1. Separation: If the soap mixture separates into layers or develops an oily film on the surface, it may not have reached trace properly. Reblend the mixture using a stick blender until it thickens and reaches trace.

2. Cloudiness: Cloudiness in liquid soap can result from incomplete saponification or the presence of impurities in the ingredients. Ensure accurate measurements and thorough mixing to prevent cloudiness.

3. pH Imbalance: If the pH of the soap is too high or too low, it may cause skin irritation. Test the pH of the soap using pH strips or a digital pH meter and adjust as needed by adding small amounts of citric acid (to lower pH) or borax solution (to raise pH).

4. Unpleasant Odor: If the soap has an unpleasant odor, it may be due to rancid oils or the presence of unreacted lye. Ensure your oils are fresh and properly stored, and double-check your measurements to ensure all the lye has reacted.

5. Hardness or Softness: The texture of the soap can vary depending on the oils used and the curing time. Adjust the oils in your recipe or extend the curing time to achieve the desired hardness or softness.

By troubleshooting these common issues and making adjustments as needed, you can ensure a successful outcome and produce high-quality liquid soap every time.

CHAPTER FIVE
ADVANCED TECHNIQUES AND FORMULATIONS

5.1 Customizing Your Recipe

Customizing your liquid soap recipe allows you to tailor the product to your preferences and needs. Here's how you can customize your recipe:

1. **Oil Selection:** Experiment with different oils to achieve various properties in your soap. For example, olive oil provides moisture and a gentle cleansing action, while coconut oil produces a rich lather. Consider factors such as skin type, desired lather, and moisturizing properties when selecting oils.

2. **Superfatting:** Adjust the superfatting percentage to customize the moisturizing properties of your soap. Superfatting involves adding extra oils to the recipe that remain unsaponified, providing additional nourishment to the skin. Higher superfat percentages result in a more moisturizing soap.

3. **Additives:** Incorporate additives such as herbs, clays, or botanical extracts to enhance the properties and appearance of your soap. For example, adding oatmeal can provide gentle exfoliation, while clay can help draw impurities from the skin.

4. Water Content: Adjust the water content in your recipe to control the consistency and hardness of the final product. More water creates a softer soap, while less water produces a harder soap.

5. Custom Blends: Create custom blends of essential oils or fragrance oils to personalize the scent of your soap. Consider the therapeutic properties of different essential oils and their compatibility with your skin when blending.

6. Special Considerations: Tailor your recipe to address specific skin concerns or preferences. For example, you can formulate a soap for sensitive skin by selecting mild oils and omitting potential irritants.

Customizing your recipe allows you to create a unique liquid soap tailored to your preferences, skin type, and desired properties.

5.2 Adding Fragrances and Colors

Adding fragrances and colors to your liquid soap can enhance its appeal and sensory experience. Here's how you can incorporate fragrances and colors into your soap:

1. Essential Oils: Choose high-quality essential oils to add natural fragrances to your soap. Essential oils not only provide pleasant scents but also offer potential therapeutic benefits for the skin and mood. Experiment with different essential oil blends to create unique scent profiles.

2. Fragrance Oils: Alternatively, you can use fragrance oils to impart specific scents to your soap. Fragrance oils offer a wide range of scent options and are often more stable than essential oils, making them suitable for long-lasting fragrance in soap.

3. Colorants: Add colorants such as natural clays, mica powders, or liquid colorants to achieve vibrant hues in your soap. Natural colorants provide a gentle, eco-friendly alternative to synthetic dyes and can add visual interest to your soap.

4. Layering and Swirling: Experiment with layering and swirling techniques to create visually stunning designs in your soap. Pour different-colored soap layers into the mold or swirl colored soap batter to achieve intricate patterns and designs.

5. Botanical Additions: Incorporate botanical additives such as dried flowers, herbs, or fruit peels to add visual interest and texture to your soap. Botanicals can also provide mild exfoliation or skin-nourishing properties.

When adding fragrances and colors to your soap, be mindful of skin sensitivities and potential allergens. Perform patch tests and use skin-safe colorants and fragrance oils to ensure the safety and quality of your finished product.

5.3 Creating Specialty Soaps

Creating specialty soaps allows you to explore unique formulations and cater to specific preferences or purposes. Here are some ideas for creating specialty soaps:

1. **Moisturizing Formulas**: Formulate moisturizing liquid soaps enriched with nourishing ingredients such as shea butter, cocoa butter, or avocado oil. These formulations provide extra hydration and protection for dry or sensitive skin.

2. **Antibacterial Blends:** Incorporate antibacterial essential oils such as tea tree, lavender, or eucalyptus to create liquid soaps with added germ-fighting properties. These formulations are ideal for handwashing and promoting cleanliness.

3. **Exfoliating Scrubs:** Create exfoliating liquid soaps infused with natural exfoliants such as ground coffee, sugar, or sea salt. These formulations gently remove dead skin cells, leaving the skin soft, smooth, and revitalized.

4. **Aromatherapy Blends:** Blend essential oils known for their aromatherapeutic properties to create liquid soaps that

promote relaxation, stress relief, or energy-boosting effects. Customize the scent profile to suit different moods and preferences.

5. Special Occasion Soaps: Design liquid soaps for special occasions or holidays by incorporating festive colors, scents, and decorative elements. These themed soaps make thoughtful gifts and add a touch of celebration to daily routines.

6. Sensitive Skin Formulations: Develop gentle liquid soaps tailored for sensitive skin by selecting mild, hypoallergenic ingredients and avoiding common irritants such as artificial fragrances and harsh detergents. When creating specialty soaps, consider the unique needs and preferences of your target audience. Experiment with different formulations, ingredients, and designs to create liquid soaps that cater to specific purposes and occasions.

CHAPTER SIX
PACKAGING AND PRESENTATION

6.1 Packaging Options

Choosing the right packaging for your liquid soap is essential for preserving its quality, enhancing its appeal, and ensuring ease of use for consumers. Here are some packaging options to consider:

1. Bottles: Selecting bottles with pumps or flip-top caps makes dispensing liquid soap convenient and mess-free. Choose bottles made from durable materials such as PET plastic or glass to protect the product from light and moisture.

2. Refill Pouches: Offer refill pouches as an eco-friendly and cost-effective option for customers to replenish their liquid soap supply. Refill pouches reduce packaging waste and are lightweight and easy to store.

3. Dispensers: Invest in refillable dispensers for bulk quantities of liquid soap, ideal for commercial or high-traffic settings such as public restrooms, schools, and offices. Dispensers come in various styles, including wall-mounted, countertop, or freestanding options.

4. Travel-Sized Containers: Provide travel-sized containers of liquid soap for customers on the go. These small, portable bottles are convenient for travel, gym bags, or handbags and allow customers to maintain cleanliness wherever they go.

5. Custom Packaging: Consider custom packaging options such as branded bottles, labels, or gift sets to differentiate your liquid soap and create a memorable brand experience for customers. Custom packaging adds a touch of professionalism and enhances brand visibility.

When selecting packaging options, prioritize functionality, durability, and eco-friendliness while aligning with your brand aesthetic and target market preferences.

6.2 Labeling Requirements

Proper labeling is crucial for communicating essential information about your liquid soap product to consumers and complying with regulatory requirements. Here are key labeling requirements to consider:

1. Product Name: Clearly state the name of the product, such as "Liquid Hand Soap" or "Moisturizing Body Wash," to indicate its intended use.

2. Ingredients List: Provide a complete list of ingredients used in the formulation, listed in descending order of predominance. Include both the common name and INCI (International Nomenclature of Cosmetic Ingredients) name for each ingredient.

3. Net Weight or Volume: Clearly indicate the net weight (for solids) or volume (for liquids) of the product in metric units (grams or milliliters).

4. Usage Instructions: Include clear instructions for use, such as how to dispense the product, how much to use, and any safety precautions or warnings.

5. Manufacturer Information: Provide the name and address of the manufacturer or distributor responsible for the product.

6. Batch Code or Lot Number: Include a batch code or lot number to facilitate traceability and quality control.

7. Expiry Date or Period After Opening (PAO): Indicate the expiry date of the product or the recommended period after opening for use. This helps consumers determine the product's freshness and shelf life.

8. Safety Information: Include any relevant safety information or warnings, such as precautions for use, storage instructions, and potential allergens.

Ensure that your product labels are legible, accurate, and compliant with applicable regulations, such as those set forth by regulatory agencies like the FDA (Food and Drug Administration) or relevant authorities in your country or region.

6.3 Presentation Ideas

Creating visually appealing presentations for your liquid soap can enhance its perceived value and attract customers' attention. Here are some presentation ideas to consider:

1. Themed Displays: Arrange your liquid soap products in themed displays that align with seasonal trends, holidays, or special promotions. For example, create a beach-themed display with shells and sand for summer or a cozy winter display with faux snow and pine cones.

2. Color Coordination: Arrange your liquid soap products by color to create visually striking displays that catch the eye. Consider grouping products by color families or creating rainbow displays for a vibrant and inviting presentation.

3. Sample Stations: Set up sample stations where customers can test and smell different liquid soap varieties before making a purchase. Provide small sample bottles or testers and encourage customers to experience the products firsthand.

4. Gift Sets and Bundles: Create gift sets or bundles featuring complementary liquid soap products paired with other items such as lotion, candles, or bath accessories. Bundle products together in attractive packaging for gift-giving occasions.

5. Interactive Demonstration : Host interactive demonstrations or workshops where customers can learn about liquid soap making techniques, ingredients, and benefits. Provide hands-on experiences and engage customers in the creative process.

6. Seasonal Decorations: Decorate your display area with seasonal decorations such as flowers, foliage, or themed props to create a festive atmosphere that reflects the time of year. Rotate decorations regularly to keep the presentation fresh and inviting.

Implementing creative presentation ideas showcase your liquid soap products effectively, capture customers' interest, and drive sales both in-store and online. Experiment with different presentation techniques to find what resonates best with your target audience and brand image.

CHAPTER SEVEN
SELLING YOUR LIQUID SOAP

7.1 Legal Considerations

Before selling your homemade liquid soap, it's essential to understand and comply with relevant legal regulations and requirements. Here are some key legal considerations to keep in mind:

1. Product Registration: In some jurisdictions, you may need to register your soap-making business and obtain permits or licenses to manufacture and sell cosmetic products. Check with local authorities or regulatory agencies to ensure compliance with legal requirements.

2. Ingredient Safety: Ensure that all ingredients used in your liquid soap formulation are safe for use in cosmetics and comply with regulations set forth by agencies such as the Food and Drug Administration (FDA) or the European Union's Cosmetic Regulation. Avoid using prohibited or restricted substances in your formulations.

3. Labeling Compliance: Follow labeling regulations for cosmetics, including requirements for listing ingredients, product net weight or volume, manufacturer contact information, and any relevant warnings or precautions. Labeling requirements may vary by region, so research and adhere to applicable guidelines.

4. Good Manufacturing Practices (GMP): Implement good manufacturing practices to ensure the safety, quality, and consistency of your liquid soap products. This includes maintaining cleanliness and hygiene in your production area, proper handling of ingredients, and adherence to standardized manufacturing procedures.

5. Product Testing and Safety Assessment: Consider conducting safety assessments or product testing, such as stability testing and microbiological testing, to ensure the safety and stability of your liquid soap formulations. Keep records of testing results and documentation to demonstrate compliance with regulatory requirements.

6. Intellectual Property Protection: Protect your brand and intellectual property by trademarking your business name, logo, or product names if desired. Be mindful of potential infringement issues and avoid using copyrighted material without permission.

By understanding and addressing legal considerations, you can minimize risks and ensure that your liquid soap business operates in compliance with applicable laws and regulations.

7.2 Marketing Strategies

Effective marketing is crucial for promoting your homemade liquid soap and attracting customers. Here are some marketing strategies to consider:

1. Identify Your Target Audience: Determine who your ideal customers are based on factors such as demographics, preferences, and buying behavior. Tailor your marketing efforts to appeal to this target audience.

2. Branding and Packaging: Develop a strong brand identity for your liquid soap business, including a memorable brand name, logo, and packaging design. Create packaging that reflects the quality and uniqueness of your products and appeals to your target market.

3. Online Presence: Establish an online presence through a professional website, social media profiles, and online marketplaces. Use these platforms to showcase your products, share engaging content, and interact with customers.

4. Content Marketing: Create valuable and informative content related to soap-making, skincare tips, or natural living to attract and engage your target audience. Consider blogging, video tutorials, or social media posts to share your expertise and build trust with potential customers.

5. Customer Reviews and Testimonials: Encourage satisfied customers to leave reviews and testimonials about your products. Positive reviews can help build credibility and trust with prospective buyers.

6. Partnerships and Collaborations: Explore partnerships with local businesses, influencers, or complementary brands to expand your reach and attract new customers. Consider collaborating on promotions, events, or product bundles to cross-promote your products.

7. Promotions and Discounts: Offer promotions, discounts, or loyalty programs to incentivize purchases and reward customer loyalty. Limited-time offers, free samples, or bundle deals can attract attention and encourage sales.

8. Networking and Community Engagement: Attend local craft fairs, farmers' markets, or community events to showcase your products and connect with potential customers face-to-face. Building relationships within your community can help generate word-of-mouth referrals and support.

By implementing a combination of these marketing strategies, you can effectively promote your homemade liquid soap and build a loyal customer base over time.

7.3 Pricing Your Product

Determining the right pricing strategy for your homemade liquid soap is essential for profitability and competitiveness. Here are some factors to consider when pricing your product:

1. Cost of Materials: Calculate the cost of ingredients, packaging, and other materials used to make each unit of liquid soap. Factor in any additional expenses such as equipment, utilities, and labor.

2. Labor and Time: Estimate the time and labor involved in making your liquid soap, including preparation, production, packaging, and administrative tasks. Consider how much your time is worth and include a fair hourly rate in your pricing.

3. Overhead Costs: Account for overhead costs associated with running your soap-making business, such as rent, utilities, insurance, and marketing expenses. Allocate a portion of these costs to each unit of liquid soap sold.

4. Competitive Analysis: Research the prices of similar liquid soap products in the market to understand pricing trends and competitive positioning. Consider how your product's quality, ingredients, branding, and value proposition compare to competitors.

5. Profit Margin: Determine your desired profit margin for each unit of liquid soap sold. This margin should cover your costs and generate a reasonable profit to reinvest in your business and sustain its growth.

6. Perceived Value: Consider the perceived value of your liquid soap products and how pricing influences consumer perceptions. Price your products competitively while maintaining quality and perceived value to attract customers.

7. Wholesale and Retail Pricing: Decide on separate pricing structures for wholesale and retail customers if you plan to sell your products through multiple channels. Wholesale pricing typically offers discounts to retailers buying in bulk.

8. Promotions and Discounts: Factor in occasional promotions, discounts, or special offers into your pricing strategy to stimulate sales and attract new customers. Be mindful of the impact of discounts on your profit margins and overall business viability.

9. Repricing and Adjustments: Regularly review and adjust your pricing strategy based on changes in costs, market demand, competition, and other relevant factors. Flexibility and adaptability are key to maintaining competitiveness in the market.

By carefully considering these factors and setting a strategic pricing strategy, you can effectively price your homemade liquid soap products to maximize profitability and appeal to your target market.

CHAPTER EIGHT
TROUBLESHOOTING COMMON ISSUES

8.1 Identifying Problems

In the process of liquid soap making, identifying problems is crucial to ensuring the quality and consistency of the final product. Here are common issues to look out for:

1. Separation: The soap mixture fails to stay emulsified, resulting in layers forming or an oily film on the surface.

2. Cloudiness: The liquid soap appears cloudy rather than clear, affecting its visual appeal.

3. pH Imbalance: The pH level of the soap is either too high or too low, potentially causing skin irritation.

4. Unpleasant Odor: The soap has an undesirable smell, indicating issues with ingredient quality or formulation.

5. Hardness or Softness: The soap is either too hard and brittle or too soft and mushy, affecting its usability.

8.2 Solutions and Fixes

Once problems are identified in the liquid soap making process, it's essential to implement effective solutions and fixes. Here are common solutions for each problem:

1. Separation:

Solution: Reblend the soap mixture thoroughly using a stick blender to ensure proper emulsification. Check and adjust the temperatures of the oils and lye solution, and add the lye solution slowly to the oils while blending.

2. Cloudiness:

Solution: Increase the mixing time or agitation during the soap-making process to ensure complete emulsification. Use distilled or filtered water to reduce impurities that can cause cloudiness. Additionally, ensure that all ingredients are fresh and of high quality.

3. pH Imbalance:

Solution: Test the pH of the soap using pH strips or a digital pH meter. If the pH is too high, add a small amount of citric acid or vinegar to lower it. If the pH is too low, add a solution of borax gradually to raise it.

4. Unpleasant Odor:

Solution: Evaluate the freshness and quality of your ingredients, especially oils and fragrances. Use fresh, high-quality ingredients, and avoid overheating oils during the melting process, which can lead to rancidity. Consider using essential oils or fragrance oils with pleasant scents.

5. Hardness or Softness:

Solution: Adjust the formulation of your soap by experimenting with different ratios of water, oils, and lye. Increasing or decreasing the amount of superfatting can also influence the texture of the soap. Explore different oil combinations to achieve the desired hardness or softness.

By promptly identifying problems and implementing effective solutions, you can ensure the quality and consistency of your homemade liquid soap and improve your soap-making skills over time.

CHAPTER NINE
TIPS FOR SUCCESS

9.1 Best Practices

When engaging in the art of liquid soap making, incorporating best practices ensures a smoother and more successful process. Here are some key best practices to enhance your liquid soap-making experience:

1. Precision in Measurements : Accurate measurement of ingredients, including oils, lye, and water, is fundamental. Use a reliable scale and measuring tools to ensure consistency and reproducibility.

2. Safety First: Prioritize safety by wearing protective gear, including gloves and goggles. Work in a well-ventilated area and exercise caution when handling lye. Follow established safety protocols to minimize risks.

3. Temperature Control: Maintain control over temperatures during the soap-making process. Monitor the temperature of oils, lye solution, and the overall mixture to achieve the desired consistency and avoid complications.

4. Thorough Mixing : Ensure thorough mixing of ingredients using a stick blender. Proper emulsification is critical to prevent issues such as separation and to achieve a smooth, homogenous liquid soap.

5. Record Keeping : Maintain detailed records of your recipes, processes, and outcomes. This helps in troubleshooting, refining formulations, and replicating successful batches.

6. Experiment Gradually : If you decide to customize your soap or try new formulations, introduce changes gradually. This allows you to observe the impact of each adjustment and avoid unexpected results.

7. Quality Ingredients : Use high-quality oils, fragrances, and additives. Fresh, premium ingredients contribute to the overall quality and effectiveness of the liquid soap.

8. Patience in Curing : Allow your liquid soap an adequate curing period. This ensures that the soap achieves its desired texture, hardness, and pH level, resulting in a more effective and pleasant product.

9. Clean Work Environment: Maintain a clean and organized workspace. This not only contributes to the safety of your soap-making process but also enhances efficiency and precision.

10. Continuous Learning : Stay informed about new techniques, ingredients, and trends in soap making. Attend workshops, join online communities, and read relevant literature to continually enhance your skills.

9.2 Helpful Resources

To support your journey in liquid soap making, explore various resources that can provide guidance, inspiration, and additional knowledge:

1. Soap Making Books: Explore well-regarded books on soap making, covering both basics and advanced techniques. Some recommended titles include "The Natural Soap Making Book for Beginners" by Kelly Cable and "Soap Crafting" by Anne-Marie Faiola.

2. Online Communities: Join online forums and communities where soap makers share experiences, tips, and troubleshooting advice. Websites like Soap Making Forum and Reddit's soapmaking subreddit are excellent platforms for learning from others in the craft.

3. YouTube Tutorials: Video tutorials on platforms like YouTube offer visual guidance for specific techniques and recipes. Channels like Soap Queen and Bramble Berry provide step-by-step demonstrations.

4. Suppliers and Specialty Stores : Establish relationships with reputable suppliers for high-quality ingredients. Specialty stores often offer workshops or resources to aid soap makers.

5. Courses and Workshops : Consider enrolling in local or online soap making courses. Many organizations and experienced soap makers offer workshops to enhance skills and share expertise.

6. Soap Making Websites: Explore websites dedicated to soap making, such as Soap Queen, Lovin Soap Studio, and Modern Soapmaking. These platforms often feature articles, recipes, and tips from experienced soap makers.

CONCLUSION

Embarking on the journey of liquid soap making opens up a world of creativity, self-expression, and functional artistry. By adhering to best practices, leveraging helpful resources, and continuously refining your skills, you can master the craft of liquid soap making. Whether it's for personal use, gifting, or potential commercial ventures, the joy of creating your own soap and the satisfaction of producing a high-quality product are truly rewarding. Remember, each batch is an opportunity to learn, experiment, and craft a soap uniquely yours. Happy soap making!

Made in the USA
Middletown, DE
20 July 2025

10901875R00029